Power from the Sun

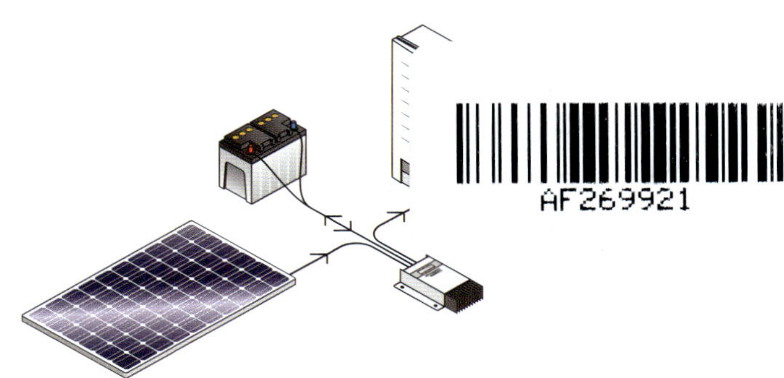

Contents **Page**

written by Suzette Toms

The sun has always been used for heating, cooking, and drying clothes.

Food like fish, corn, and fruit can be dried in the sun. Then it is ready to eat for a long time. Flowers can be dried in the sun, too.

Now solar energy can be used to make electricity.

Power from the sun is clean energy. It doesn't make a mess, and it will never run out. The sun will always be there.

We know that the sun doesn't shine at night! Bad weather can stop the sunlight, too.

Solar power doesn't always work well.

Solar power can cost
a lot of money.
It gives us only a
little bit of the world's
electricity now. But this
is changing. The sun's
power can be used to
make small things go.

solar calculator

When you turn on a light, power moves
through the wires to make it go.
It can make your house warm, and give
you hot water.

solar light

Solar cells make power from the sun for you to use. Some day it could be the power for cars and planes.

solar cell

Solar power will get better
and better. Soon it will be
ready for everyone to use.
It will make lots of things go.

roof panels

Power from the sun is one of
the best ways to help our world.